MICROCOS

Microcosm Publishing is Portland's most diversified publishing house and distributor with a focus on the colorful, authentic, and empowering. Our books and zines have put your power in your hands since 1996, equipping readers to make positive changes in their lives and in the world around them. Microcosm emphasizes skill-building, showing hidden histories, and fostering creativity through challenging conventional publishing wisdom with books and bookettes about DIY skills, food, bicycling, gender, self-care, and social justice. What was once a distro and record label was started by Joe Biel in his bedroom and has become among the oldest independent publishing houses in Portland, OR. We are a politically moderate, centrist publisher in a world that has inched to the right for the past 80 years.

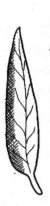

Healing Your Magical Body with Plants + Minerals

ALL CONTENT IS © 2012
JO-JO SHERROW

CONTENTS

INTRO

* THIS BOOK IS A REFERENCE FOR ADDRESSING VARIOUS HEALTH ISSUES AND ORGAN SYSTEMS WITHIN THE BODY WITH HERBS. I HAVE LISTED MY PERSONAL FAVORITES AND ONES THAT I AM FAMILIAR WITH. THIS LIST IS NOT EXHAUSTIVE. PLEASE FEEL FREE AND GET EXCITED ABOUT RESEARCHING EACH HERB THOUROUGHLY ON THE WEB AND CONSULT A HANDFUL OF BOOKS, SO YOU ARE FAMILIAR WITH HOW THE PLANT LOOKS, WHAT ITS PARTICULAR QUALITIES ARE, AND WHAT SYSTEM(S) IT HAS AN AFFINITY FOR.

* BE OPEN TO TRYING A FEW DIFFERENT HERBS SEPARATELY TO FIND OUT WHAT YOUR BODY/MIND LIKES AND WHAT IT DOESN'T. FOR EXAMPLE, FOR LIVER ISSUES, SOME PEOPLE LIKE BITTER LEAVES SUCH AS WORMWOOD. OTHERS PREFER ROOTS LIKE BURDOCK OR DANDELION. THE POINT IS, YOU DON'T KNOW UNTIL YOU TRY. LISTEN TO YOUR BODY. SEE HOW S/HE REACTS. AND MOST OF ALL, HAVE FUN!

EACH PLANT HAS ITS OWN PARTICULAR WISDOM THAT IT IS DIRECTLY PASSING TO YOU WHEN YOU HAPPILY PARTAKE OF IT. LISTEN FOR THE WISDOM. BE OPEN TO IT, THEN SHARE THE LOVE AND TALK ABOUT IT WITH OTHERS. THE PLANTS AND PLANT LOVERS WILL THANK YOU FOR IT.

- JOJO SHERROW, 2011

INTRO TO THE SECOND EDITION

THE LOVE AND ATTENTION WE GIVE TO
TECHNOLOGY AND MACHINES CAN
BE BALANCED BY AN INCREASED LOVE
AND APPRECIATION FOR THE PLANT
KINGDOM. WHAT BETTER WAY TO
BECOME RECONNECTED TO THIS WORLD
AND ITS RHYTHMS THAN BY MAKING YOUR
OWN MEDICINES AND SKIN CARE WITH
* PLANTS YOU HAVE GROWN YOURSELF
OR THOSE YOU HAVE FORAGED IN THE
LOCAL PARK OR WOODS CLOSE TO HOME.

IN THE NEW EDITION OF THIS BOOK,
I HAVE ADDED 20 NEW PAGES WITH
INFORMATION ON ADDITIONAL SYSTEMS
OF THE BODY AND THEIR HERBAL/PLANT
COUNTER PARTS. PLUS THERE ARE
NEW PAGES DEDICATED TO MAKING
MORE MEDICINES AND YOUR OWN
SKIN CARE AND PERFUME.

LET'S ENJOY TOGETHER AND
APPRECIATE WHAT THE WONDROUS
PLANT AND DEVIC WORLD HAS
TO SHARE

— JoJo SHERROW
5/2012

* GROWN IN CONTAINERS
ON YOUR FIRE ESCAPE,
KITCHEN WINDOW BOX,
ROOF, DECK, OR PATIO.

TEETH + GUMS

WE CAN SUPPORT THE STRENGTH
OF OUR TOOTH ENAMEL WITH
ADEQUATE CALCIUM + VITAMIN D
INTAKE. ASIDE FROM THAT, THERE
ARE MANY PLANTS THAT HAVE AN
AFFINITY FOR OUR INCISORS,
CANINES, + MOLARS.

OIL PULLING TECHNIQUE

THIS WILL **STRENGTHEN** AND
WHITEN THE TEETH. THE IDEA BEHIND
IT IS THAT COCONUT OIL ACTS AS A
SOLVENT THAT **DISSOLVES** PLAQUE.

1 tsp COCONUT OIL
* SWISH THROUGH TEETH, GUMS, AND
  MOUTH FOR 1 *full* MINUTE.
  (THINK OF THIS AS AN OIL MOUTHWASH)

SAGE - CHEWING SAGE LEAVES WILL
CUT DOWN ON CAVITY FORMING
BACTERIA LIVING IN THE MOUTH

* BREW A STRONG SAGE TEA
  TO GARGLE WITH + USE AS
  A MOUTHWASH.

2 tsp DRIED SAGE LEAVES] STEEP
1 C. water BOILING   ] 1 HOUR

PEPPERMINT - IS ANOTHER ANTI-BACTERIAL
HERB WITH AN AFFINITY FOR THE
TEETH AND GUMS.
* TRY THIS MINTY MOUTHWASH

1 OZ VODKA
1 OZ VEGETABLE GLYCERINE
2 DROPS PEPPERMINT ESSENTIAL OIL

MIX TOGETHER ALL INGREDIENTS.
STORE IN A GLASS BOTTLE OR JAR
* * *

DIGESTION

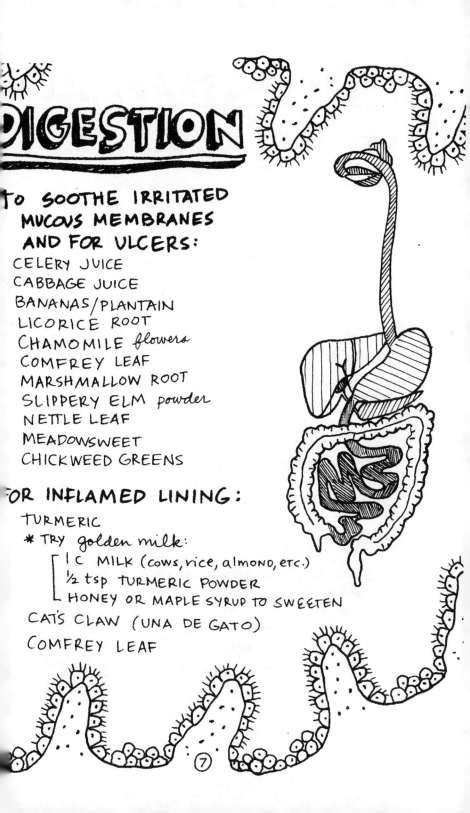

TO SOOTHE IRRITATED
   MUCOUS MEMBRANES
   AND FOR ULCERS:
CELERY JUICE
CABBAGE JUICE
BANANAS/PLANTAIN
LICORICE ROOT
CHAMOMILE *flowers*
COMFREY LEAF
MARSHMALLOW ROOT
SLIPPERY ELM *powder*
NETTLE LEAF
MEADOWSWEET
CHICKWEED GREENS

FOR INFLAMED LINING:
   TURMERIC
   * TRY *golden milk:*
      [I C MILK (cows, rice, almond, etc.)
      ½ tsp TURMERIC POWDER
      HONEY OR MAPLE SYRUP TO SWEETEN
   CAT'S CLAW (UNA DE GATO)
   COMFREY LEAF

STOMACH / SPLEEN

FOODS to SOOTHE:

ROOT VEGGIES
  CARROTS
  TURNIPS
  RUTABAGA
  PARSNIPS
RICE
MOCHI (BAKED SWEET rice)
COCONUT MILK
KABOCHA SQUASH
AVOCADO
APPLESAUCE
MANGO

try this: KITCHAREE

- ⅓ C. SUNFLOWER SEEDS   ½ tsp SALT
- ⅓ C. LENTILS
- ⅓ C, RICE
- ¼ C. FRESH CILANTRO (GARNISH)
- ½ tsp TURMERIC
- 2 C WATER

COOK MIXTURE FOR ½ HOUR.
GARNISH WITH CILANTRO AND
FLAX OR HEMP SEED OIL.

THIS WAY TO THE STOMACH!

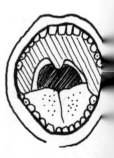

THE BOWELS

CONSTIPATION (COLON RELAXERS, AND PERISTALSIS PROMOTING HERBS)

- PSYLLIUM SEEDS
- SLIPPERY ELM BARK
- SENNA PODS * STRONG LAXATIVE
- GROUND FLAX SEEDS OR FLAX SEED TEA
- LICORICE   ↳ SPRINKLE ON FOOD
- FENNEL
- CINNAMON
- DANDELION
- BURDOCK
- MARSHMALLOW

THE COLON

TO CURB DIARRHEA

- NETTLE LEAF
- SEAWEED *broth* (KELP, KOMBU, DULSE)
- RED RASPBERRY LEAF
- SHEEP'S SORREL
- SLIPPERY ELM
- YELLOW DOCK
- OAK BARK
- APPLESAUCE
- CINNAMON
- BANANAS
- COMFREY LEAF

 # LIVER — WE GENERATE A NEW LIVER EVERY SIX WEEKS!

TONICS:

MOST BITTER HERBS ARE TONIFYING TO THE LIVER AND HELP TO STIMULATE BILE WHICH IS CONCENTRATED AND STORED IN THE GALL BLADDER UNTIL IT IS NEEDED TO AID IN THE DIGESTION OF FATS.

DANDELION *root*
BURDOCK *root*
MILK THISTLE *seeds*
BLESSED THISTLE
OREGON GRAPE *root*
GENTIAN *root*

ROSEMARY
TURMERIC
PARSLEY

SOOTHE WITH FOODS:

CELERY
SESAME SEEDS
KELP
NORI
PLUMS
MULBERRIES

COOL LIVER
DAIKON
CELERY
CUCUMBER
ARUGULA
CARROTS
RADISH

EGGPLANT
LEEKS/SCALLIONS/CHIVES
COCONUT MILK
CHESTNUTS
BLACK PEPPER
CABBAGE

MOVE LIVER CHI

KIDNEY

THE KIDNEYS ARE COMPOSED OF MILLIONS OF TINY UNITS CALLED **NEPHRONS**. KIDNEYS REGULATE THE BODY'S WATER, SALT, AND CHEMICAL CONTENT.

ADRENAL GLANDS: ARE GLANDS THAT SIT ATOP OF THE KIDNEYS AND CREATE HORMONES SUCH AS ADRENALIN WHICH IS INVOLVED IN THE "FIGHT OR FLIGHT" RESPONSE. PRACTICE RELAXING ENERGETICALLY THE KIDNEY AREA TO INVOKE THE PARASYMPATHETIC NERVOUS SYSTEM, INVOLVED IN RELAXATION AND DIGESTION.

HERBS:

ROSE HIPS
GOLDENROD
CLEAVERS *leaf*
NETTLE LEAF
ECHINACEA *root*
MARSHMALLOW ROOT
ELEUTHERO GINSENG
LICORICE
SARSAPARILLA

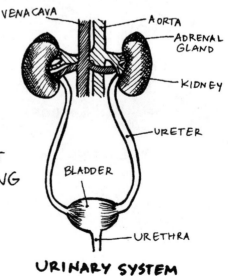

URINARY SYSTEM

UTERINE REPRODUCTIVE SYSTEM

ENDO-METRIUM — UTERUS — CERVIX — OVARY — FALLOPIAN TUBE — VAGINA

REGULATING THE MENSTRUAL CYCLE:

HERE ARE A FEW FOODS/HERBS THAT PROMOTE ESTROGEN + F.S.H.* DAY 1-14 AND PROMOTE PROGESTERONE + L.H.* FOR DAYS 15-28.

DAY 1-14

FLAX OIL (1-2 TBS/day)
MACA - STIMULATES GRAAFIAN FOLLICLES

DAY 15-28

HEMP SEED OIL (1-2 TBS/day)
EVENING PRIMROSE OIL (1300 mg/day)
WILD YAM (1 c. tea/day or 1/4 tsp tincture)
CHASTE TREE (1/4 tsp. TINCTURE/day)

TONICS:

YARROW
SASSAFRAS
CINNAMON
ORANGE PEEL

DAY 1 = MENSTRUATION
↳ DAY 14 = OVULATION

* FOLLICLE STIMULATING HORMONE
* LUTENIZING HORMONE

12

CRAMPS: *herbs for*
- RED RASPBERRY
- CRAMP BARK
- MOTHERWORT
- SKULLCAP
- VALERIAN
- BLACK HAW

TO BRING ON A DELAYED PERIOD:
- MUGWORT
- PENNYROYAL
- MOTHERWORT
- OSHA
- LEMON BALM
- GINGER
- HYSSOP
- DAMIANA

TO CURB EXCESS FLOW:
- LADY'S MANTLE
- SHEPHERD'S PURSE

MEN-O-PAUSE *allies*:
- DONG QUAI
- CHASTE TREE (VITEX)
- LICORICE
- GINGER
- SAGE
- SARSAPARILLA
- SPIRULINA
- PANAX GINSENG
- POMEGRANATE

LUNAR CALENDAR

JANUARY	1 2 3 4 5 6 7 8 9 10 11 12 13 14 15 16 17 18 19 20 21 22 23 24 25 26 27 28 29 30 31
FEBRUARY	1 2 3 4 5 6 7 8 9 10 11 12 13 14 15 16 17 18 19 20 21 22 23 24 25 26 27 28
MARCH	1 2 3 4 5 6 7 8 9 10 11 12 13 14 15 16 17 18 19 20 21 22 23 24 25 26 27 28 29 30 31
APRIL	1 2 3 4 5 6 7 8 9 10 11 12 13 14 15 16 17 18 19 20 21 22 23 24 25 26 27 28 29 30
MAY	1 2 3 4 5 6 7 8 9 10 11 12 13 14 15 16 17 18 19 20 21 22 23 24 25 26 27 28 29 30 31
JUNE	1 2 3 4 5 6 7 8 9 10 11 12 13 14 15 16 17 18 19 20 21 22 23 24 25 26 27 28 29 30
JULY	1 2 3 4 5 6 7 8 9 10 11 12 13 14 15 16 17 18 19 20 21 22 23 24 25 26 27 28 29 30 31
AUGUST	1 2 3 4 5 6 7 8 9 10 11 12 13 14 15 16 17 18 19 20 21 22 23 24 25 26 27 28 29 30 31
SEPTEMBER	1 2 3 4 5 6 7 8 9 10 11 12 13 14 15 16 17 18 19 20 21 22 23 24 25 26 27 28 29 30
OCTOBER	1 2 3 4 5 6 7 8 9 10 11 12 13 14 15 16 17 18 19 20 21 22 23 24 25 26 27 28 29 30 31
NOVEMBER	1 2 3 4 5 6 7 8 9 10 11 12 13 14 15 16 17 18 19 20 21 22 23 24 25 26 27 28 29 30
DECEMBER	1 2 3 4 5 6 7 8 9 10 11 12 13 14 15 16 17 18 19 20 21 22 23 24 25 26 27 28 29 30 31

● = New Moon

= Full Moon

(14)

PENILE REPRODUCTIVE SYSTEM

TONIC + RESTORATIVE HERBS

PANAX GINSENG *root* – TINCTURE
MACA ROOT – POWDER
SARSAPARILLA – TEA
CARDAMOM – TEA
OAT STRAW – TINCTURE OR TEA
ASHWAGANDA – TEA

URINARY TRACT INFECTIONS

USNEA – TINCTURE (USNEA IS A LICHEN!)
CRANBERRY – CAPSULES OR UNSWEETENED JUICE
PLAIN SEA SALT BATHS
½ LEMON SQUEEZED IN WATER UPON WAKING.

FOR PROSTATE HEALTH

SAW PALMETTO *berry*
RED CLOVER *blossom*
NETTLE *root*
CLEAVERS

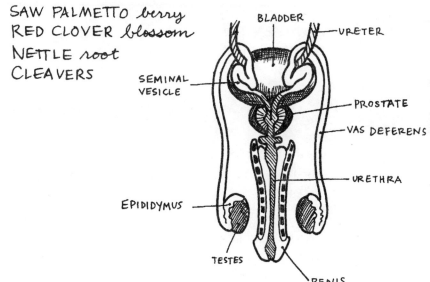

BLADDER
URETER
SEMINAL VESICLE
PROSTATE
VAS DEFERENS
URETHRA
EPIDIDYMUS
TESTES
PENIS

CONNECTIVE TISSUE
AND

HAIR: NETTLE LEAF, SAGE(GREEN), NEEM, ROSEMARY OIL, COCONUT OIL, HENNA

SKIN: CALENDULA, ST. JOHNS WORT—OIL

NAILS: INFUSION NEEM

BONES: COMFREY LEAF

ECZEMA PSORIASIS RASHES DERMATITIS

JOINTS: DEVIL'S CLAW, TURMERIC, ROSEMARY, CAT'S CLAW, NETTLE LEAF, SAGE, MEADOWSWEET

for ARTHRITIS RELIEF

CUTS/SCRAPES:

	PARTS	
GOLDENSEAL	1	COMBINE + PACK INTO CUT
SLIPPERY ELM	3	PLACE ON CUT +
(POWDERS)		COVER W/A BANDAGE.

* AFTER A SCAB FORMS, COVER W/MASHED BANANA RECOVER W/BANDAGE.

COMMON PLANTAIN (Plantago major) IS <u>THE</u> PLANT FOR CUTS, SCRAPES, AND INSECT BITES.
* PICK A FEW FRESH LEAVES (THESE ARE UBIQUITOUS IN MOST OF N. AMERICA). CHEW THE LEAVES THEN APPLY THE LEAVES TO THE CUT. COVER WITH A BAND-AID.

muscles—
ARNICA—
CREAM OR OIL FOR
KAVA KAVA—
SALVE

THE **THYROID** gland

THE THYROID GLAND IS LINKED TO OUR
5TH CHAKRA (THE THROAT CHAKRA). ITS
COLOR IS SKY BLUE.
THYROID ISSUES ARE SUPPORTED BY
* SINGING IN THE SHOWER
* VOCALIZING
* WRITING
* SPEAKING **YOUR** TRUTH
* SPEAKING FROM YOUR ♡
* WEAR AN AQUAMARINE CRYSTAL PENDANT
* TAKE AQUAMARINE GEM ESSENCE
* MASSAGE FEET AND/OR BODY
  WITH ONE OF THE FLORAL
  OILS DESCRIBED ON   p.35 + p.38.

HERBS TO SUPPORT THE thyroid

HYPO- thyroid
BLADDERWRACK
NETTLE
ELEUTHERO GINSENG (TINCTURE)
BLACK PEPPER
SEAWEED (DULSE, WAKAME, NORI)

HYPER- thyroid
BUGLEWEED
MOTHERWORT
LEMON BALM
CHICKWEED

LUNGS

BREATHE IN, BREATHE OUT

BRONCHIO-DILATORS
OSHA ROOT
MULLEIN - SOOTHING + ASTRINGENT
ELCAMPANE - TONIC + EXPECTORANT

EXPECTORANTS
HOREHOUND
WILD CHERRY BARK
BASIL/TULSI

THYME
HYSSOP
RED CLOVER
blossoms

TO SOOTHE COUGHS
SLIPPERY ELM
COLTSFOOT - EXPECTORANT + SOOTHING

try a smoking blend:
KINNICK KINNICK

OSHA
MULLEIN
RED WILLOW   COMBINE IN
UVA URSI   EQUAL PARTS
YERBA SANTE

02 GARLIC + ONION COUGH SYRUP:

1 small ONION   CHOP GARLIC + ONION.
5 CLOVES OF GARLIC   COMBINE IN A
3/4 c. HONEY   GLASS JAR. LET
                       SIT FOR A DAY OR TWO.
                       TAKE A SPOONFUL
                       3-4 TIMES PER DAY.

ALLERGIES

A-CHOO!

ZIE GAZUNT.

EXPERIMENT WITH THE FOLLOWING FOODS AND HERBS TO SEE IF THEY ALLEVIATE SOME OF THE HISTAMINE REACTIONS YOU MAY BE EXPERIENCING FROM AN ALLERGEN.

#1 NETTLE LEAF!
   GREEN TEA
   BUTTERBUR
   SAGE
   YARROW

LEMONGRASS
BEE POLLEN (LOCAL)
CAYENNE
EYEBRIGHT
ROSEMARY
RAW HONEY

THE SINUSES

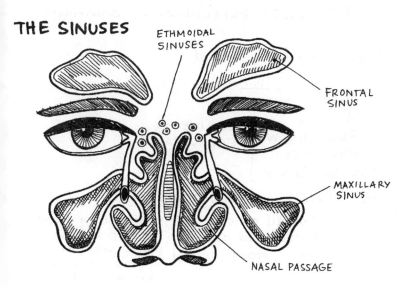

ETHMOIDAL SINUSES

FRONTAL SINUS

MAXILLARY SINUS

NASAL PASSAGE

FLU + COLDS

*HERE ARE 3 CATEGORIES OF HERBS TO EXPERIMENT WITH WHEN EXPERIENCING THE FLU OR A WINTER COLD.

IMMUNE STRENGTHENERS:

ASTRAGALUS root - TINCTURE OR TEA
ECHINACEA root - ALCOHOL OR GLYCERITE TINCTURE
REISHI mushroom - TINCTURE

ANTI-VIRALS:

ST. JOHN'S WORT - TEA
LEMON BALM - TEA
HYSSOP - TEA
BONESET - TINCTURE
ECHINACEA - TINCTURE

TO DECONGEST:

GINGER	HORSERADISH / WASABI
PEPPERMINT	NETTLE
THYME	ELDER FLOWER
SAGE	YARROW flower
GOLDENSEAL	ELDER berry

try: HOT GINGER-ROSE lemonade
1 T ROSE BUDS
1 T FRESH CHOPPED GINGER   1 PT BOILING WATER
½ A LEMON, JUICED

THE BODY'S
ELECTRICAL SYSTEM

AKA THE
NERVOUS
SYSTEM

NEURON- A CELL THAT REACTS TO
AN ELECTRIC CHARGE. IT PROCESSES
AND TRANSMITS INFO BY ELECTRICAL
AND CHEMICAL SIGNALING.

AXON- A PROJECTING FIBER OF A NEURON.

SYNAPSE- SPACE BETWEEN AN AXON
TERMINAL AND A NEURON.

DENDRITE- THE BRANCHED
PROJECTIONS OF A NEURON.

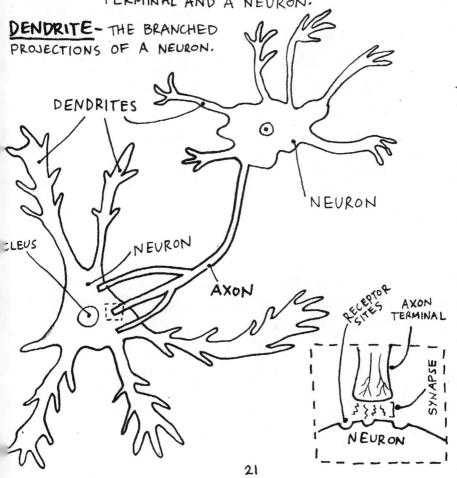

DENDRITES

NEURON

CLEUS

NEURON

AXON

RECEPTOR SITES

AXON TERMINAL

SYNAPSE

NEURON

21

MENTAL HEALTH tonics

AND THE NERVOUS SYSTEM

PASSION FLOWER ♡♡ -TEA

SKULLCAP ♡♡ -TEA

KAVA KAVA ♡♡♡ -TEA

VALERIAN ♡♡ -GLYCERITE TINCTURE

CATMINT ♡ - TEA

CHAMOMILE ♡ -TEA

LINDEN ♡♡ -TEA

VERVAIN ♡ -TEA

ROSE ♡ -OIL

ST. JOHN'S WORT ♡♡ OIL

HOPS ♡♡ -HERBAL PILL

LAVENDER ♡ HERBAL PILLOW OR ESSENTIAL OIL PERFUME (p.40)

MOST OF THE ABOVE PLANTS WILL ACT AS NERVOUS SYSTEM RESTORATIVES AND/OR TONICS. ANXIETY, DEPRESSION, AND INSOMNIA MAY ALL BE ADDRESSED USING ANY OF THESE PLANTS. TRY 1 FOR A WEEK TO SEE ITS EFFECT ON YOUR PARTICULAR BODY/MIND. TRY OTHERS IN THE SAME WAY. BLEND A FEW TOGETHER WHEN YOU FIND OUT WHICH ONES ARE YOUR FAVORITES.

♡ = MILD
♡♡ = MEDIUM
♡♡♡ = STRONG
} HERB STRENGTH!

22

MINERALS

SILICA (SiO_2)

IS FOUND IN:

STRAWBERRIES
WATERMELLON
OATS/OATSTRAW.
HORSETAIL
SPRING WATER

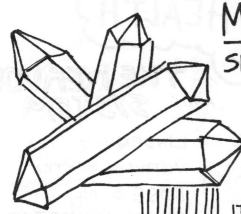

ITS MOLECULAR
STRUCTURE IS SIMILAR
TO QUARTZ CRYSTAL.

MINERALS ENCOURAGE
ALKALINIZATION
OF THE BODY.

FERMENTED FOODS
CONTAIN MINERALS
MORE READILY
AVAILABLE ON
ACCOUNT OF
ACIDS +
GOOD
BACTERIA.

SILICA + QUARTZ
ARE PIZO-ELECTRIC.
THAT IS, THEY SEND AN
ELECTRIC CURRENT (SIGNAL)
UNDER A CERTAIN
TEMPERATURE AND
PRESSURE.

SILICA IS ESSENTIAL
FOR THE GROWTH OF
HAIR, SKIN AND NAILS.
IT ALSO IS PROTECTIVE
AGAINST E.M.F.s - THE
(ELECTRO-MAGNETIC
FREQUENCY) OF CELL PHONES
AND COMPUTERS.

$(NaCl)$
SEA SALT -

SEA SALT HAS A
PURIFYING EFFECT
ON THE BODY WHEN
TAKEN INTERNALLY IN SMALL
AMOUNTS + WHEN TAKING
A SALT BATH.

23

PARASITIC INFECTIONS

- THESE CRITTERS CAN INVADE THE HUMAN BODY VIA THE SURFACE OF THE SKIN (EXTERNALLY) OR THE DIGESTIVE SYSTEM/MUCOSAL LINING (INTERNALLY).

- A PARTICULARLY UBIQUITOUS ORGANISM BY THE NAME OF TINEA CRURIS FUNGUS IS RESPONSIBLE FOR RINGWORM, ATHLETE'S FOOT, AND JOCK ITCH. THEIR IDEAL ENVIRONMENT IS WARM, DARK, AND SWEATY. WHEN ADDRESSING THESE ISSUES, CREATE AN UNFIT SPACE FOR THESE NASTY MICRO-BEASTS BY DUSTING THE SKIN WITH THE FOLLOWING POWDER:

EXTERNAL

- 1 tsp BLACK WALNUT HULL powder
- 2 T CORNSTARCH
- 1 tsp GOLDEN SEAL POWDER
- 1 tsp CALENDULA FLOWERS
- ¼ c. FRENCH GREEN CLAY POWDER
- 2 drops LAVENDER OIL
- 2 drops TEA TREE OIL
- 1 tsp CALAMINE POWDER

* MIX TOGETHER + STORE IN AN AIR-TIGHT CONTAINER. APPLY TO DRY SKIN MORNING + NIGHT.

OTHERS TO TRY TOPICALLY

WITCH HAZEL   IODINE
ALOE GEL
JEWEL WEED

PARASITES/WORMS/FUNGUS

INTERNAL INFECTIONS SHOW UP AS
TAPE WORMS, ROUND WORMS, PINWORMS
AND CERTAIN PESKY PROTOZOA.

THE FOLLOWING ARE
<u>VERMIFUGES</u> - ANYTHING THAT WORKS
   TO EXPEL INTESTINAL WORMS:

   PAPAIN (PAPAYA ENZYMES) - CAPSULE FORM
   NEEM - TINCTURE
   BLACK WALNUT HULLS - TINCTURE
   PINEAPPLE - FRESH
   CLOVES - CHEW A FEW PER DAY
   WORMWOOD - TINCTURE
   GARDEN GREEN SAGE - FRESH
   GUM ARABIC - RENDERS THE
      INTESTINAL MUCOSA LESS EASY
      FOR WORMS TO LIVE ON/IN
         * 1/4 tsp OF THE POWDER
               IN WARM H_2O ONCE
               PER DAY IN THE AM.
   GARLIC - CAPSULE, FRESH, OR COOKED

   PSYLLIUM - SEEDS <u>OR</u> HUSKS
      1/2 tsp PER DAY ON AN EMPTY STOMACH
      1st SOAK THEM IN 1/4 C. OF WATER

GROW A POTTED PLANT OF **RUE** (Ruta graveolens)
   CHEW 1 LEAF CLUSTER PER DAY

GROW SOME **THYME**
   ADD FRESH TO COOKED FOODS
   AND SALAD DRESSINGS

INTERNAL

25

HEAVY METALS

WE ARE IN CONTACT WITH MANY DIFFERENT METALS ON A DAILY BASIS. WE HAVE MERCURY FILLINGS, ALUMINUM FOOD CONTAINERS, LEAD SOLDER IN OUR WATER PIPES (SOMETIMES), PLUS OTHER HIDDEN SOURCES. TO HELP THE BODY CARRY THESE PESKY MOLECULES + PARTICLES OUT OF THE SYSTEM WE CAN INCLUDE THE FOLLOWING IN OUR DIET:

BURDOCK ROOT (INFUSION)   SPIRULINA

SEAWEED → DULSE – AS A SNACK
- NORI
- KELP
- KOMBU   ] IN SOUPS
- WAKAME

MUSHROOMS → SHIITAKE] IN SOUPS
- MAITAKE
- CHAGA – TINCTURE
- REISHI – TINCTURE

CILANTRO (FRESH OR COOKED LEAVES)

BLACK TOURMALINE
YARROW   ] *flower* + GEM ESSENCES
AMETHYST

* TRY *radiate* LOVE *soup*

3T SUSHI RICE	BRING TO A
3C WATER	BOIL, TURN HEAT
5 SHIITAKES	DOWN TO SIMMER.
½ tsp SALT	COOK FOR 1 HOUR.
¼ C WAKAME	GARNISH WITH:
2 carrots	CILANTRO + DULSE !

HOW TO APPROACH PLANTS

IF YOU ARE NEW TO EXPERIMENTING
WITH PLANTS AS TRANSFORMATIONAL
VEHICLES TO FACILLITATE WELL BEING,
START WITH 1 PLANT ALLY OR COMBINATION.
THIS METHOD WILL GIVE YOUR BODY
A CHANCE TO TELL YOU WITH ITS
SOMATIC CUES IF THE PLANT YOU ARE
INGESTING IN TEA OR TINCTURE FORM OR
APPLYING EXTERNALLY AS AN OIL IS A
VIBRATIONAL MATCH WITH YOUR
PARTICULAR SYSTEM. THINK OF IT THIS
WAY, YOU MEET MANY PEOPLE DURING
YOUR LIFE ON EARTH, PROBABLY IN THE
THOUSANDS. YET ONLY ABOUT A FEW DOZEN
(GIVE OR TAKE) BECOME YOUR CLOSEST
FRIENDS. FRIENDS RESONATE WITH YOU
AS DO HERBS. SO MAKE IT YOUR GOAL
TO HAVE A FEW BFFs IN THE
PLANT KINGDOM THAT YOU CAN
LEAN ON FOR SUPPORT. IF YOU TAKE
AN HERB AND EITHER SEE NO RESULTS OR
FEEL BADLY AFTER A FEW DAYS, STOP TAKING IT.
ACCEPT THAT THIS IS NOT ONE OF YOUR
ALLIES AND MOVE ON TO THE NEXT
HERB YOU HAVE AN AFFINITY FOR.

SMOOTHIES

SMOOTHIES ARE AN EASY WAY TO
INCORPORATE NUTRIENT DENSITY
INTO YOUR DIET.

* HERE ARE SOME NOT SO COMMON DELICIOUS
ADDITIONS TO THE USUAL SUSPECTS.

AVOCADO
RAW CACAO POWDER
BEE POLLEN - BUY LOCAL @ YOUR
FARMER'S MARKET
FLAX OIL
HEMP OIL
SEA SALT
SPIRULINA POWDER
ACAI
CHIA SEEDS
PSYLLIUM SEEDS
TURMERIC ⎤
CINNAMON ⎥ POWDER
GINGER ⎦

MIX-N-MATCH WITH FRUIT/MILK/JUICE

STRAWBERRY
BLUEBERRY
BANANA
MANGO

ORANGE JUICE
YOGURT
RICE/HEMP MILK

HERBAL INFUSIONS

(ANOTHER NAME FOR A STRONG TEA)

STANDARD DOSAGE OF DRIED
ROOTS, LEAVES, FLOWERS OR SEEDS:

1 teaspoon HERBS
1 c. boiling WATER

WEEEEE!

CUP

SPOON

KETTLE

STEEPING TIMES:

ROOTS	8 HRS HOURS
LEAVES	1-4 HRS
FLOWERS	20 MINUTES
SEEDS	30 MINUTES
BARKS	4-8 HOURS

* IF PRESSED FOR TIME, A 15 MINUTE INFUSION WILL WORK AS WELL, BUT YOUR TEA WON'T BE AS STRONG.

* TRY MAKING YOUR INFUSIONS BEFORE BEDTIME AND LET STEEP OVER NIGHT. YOUR TEA WILL BE WAITING FOR YOU IN THE MORNING.

TRY USING A QUART SIZE MASON JAR TO BREW A LARGE AMOUNT OF TEA.
2-3 TABLESPOONS OF HERBS
1 QT BOILING WATER
CAP LOOSELY WITH LID.
STEEP FOR THE APPROPRIATE TIME.

TINCTURES + GLYCERITES

A TINCTURE IS AN ALCOHOL BASED
EXTRACT OF A FRESH OR DRIED PLANT'S
LEAVES, ROOTS, OR FLOWERS.
WHILE ALCOHOL TINCTURES ARE THE
MOST COMMON, OTHER LIQUIDS SUCH
AS APPLE CIDER VINEGAR OR
GLYCERINE ARE USED.

FRESH GINGER TINCTURE

WHAT YOU WILL NEED:

2 OZ BABY FOOD JAR W/A LID
PYREX MEASURING CUP
2 OZ VODKA
MEDIUM SIZED GINGER ROOT (FRESH)
UNBLEACHED CHEESE CLOTH

DIRECTIONS:

1st CHOP YOUR FRESH GINGER
ROOT INTO SMALL PIECES.
FILL THE JAR ABOUT 75%.
NEXT POUR ALCOHOL TO FILL THE
JAR COMPLETELY. CAP TIGHTLY AND
STORE IN A DRY CUPBOARD FOR
ABOUT 6 WEEKS. AFTER 6 WEEKS,
DECANT THE LIQUID INTO THE
MEASURING CUP, FILTERED THROUGH
THE CHEESE CLOTH.

TINCTURES (CONT'D)

SQUEEZE OUT ANY REMAINING TINCTURE
LIQUID. NEXT, TRANSFER THE TINCTURE TO
A BROWN OR BLUE GLASS BOTTLE WITH
A PIPETTE DROPPER FOR DOSAGES.

LABEL THE BOTTLE WITH
THE NAME + DATE

"GINGER TINCTURE
IN VODKA
5/20/12"

BABY FOOD JAR
LABEL GOES ON
LID.
USE A SHARPIE.
(IT'S WATERPROOF!)

INFUSED OILS

INFUSED OILS CAN BE USED AS A
MASSAGE OIL OR AS AN INGREDIENT
IN LIP BALM, OINTMENTS, SALVES
AND CREAMS. THE PROCESS TO
MAKE THE OIL IS SIMILAR TO THAT
OF A TINCTURE. THE MAIN DIFFERENCE
IS THE IMPORTANCE OF CREATING AN
AIRTIGHT ENVIRONMENT FOR THE
HERB TO EXTRACT IN. CHECK EVERY
SO OFTEN FOR AIR BUBBLES AND
POP THEM / ADD MORE OIL AS NECESSARY.

INFUSED OILS

VIOLET LEAF OIL *

2 OZ OLIVE OR GRAPESEED OIL

~ 1 CUP FRESH VIOLET LEAVES

2 OZ GLASS BABY FOOD JAR

FIRST MAKE SURE THE JAR IS CLEAN AND COMPLETELY DRY. A WATER DROPLET COULD BE BAD NEWS FOR THE OIL. IT'S RECOMMENDED TO BOIL OR STERILIZE THE JAR USING YOUR DISHWASHER.

NEXT CHOP THE FRESH LEAVES INTO VERY SMALL PIECES WITH A SHARP KNIFE OR TEAR WITH YOUR HANDS, PREFERABLY WHILE SINGING. THIS SETS THE SPACE AND ENERGY FIELD FOR AN OIL WITH A HIGH VIBRATIONAL FREQUENCY.

THEN COVER THE LEAVES WITH OIL. MAKE SURE YOU FILL THE OIL TO THE TOP OF THE JAR. WE WANT TO CREATE AN AIR-TIGHT ENVIRONMENT TO DISCOURAGE MOLD GROWTH.

PLACE THE JAR IN A CUPBOARD AND LET SIT FOR **5** WEEKS.

AFTER 5 WEEKS, DECANT OIL INTO A MEASURING CUP USING CHEESE CLOTH AS A FILTER.

> * VIOLET LEAF OIL IS USED OFTEN TO ADDRESS THE ISSUE OF **CYSTIC BREASTS.**

INFUSED OILS (CONT'D)

STORE YOUR OIL IN A GLASS JAR AND AWAY FROM THE SUNLIGHT. OILS OF ANY KIND ARE EXTREMELY PHOTO-SENSITIVE AND WILL LOSE THEIR POTENCY IF EXPOSED TO THE SUN.

SALVES, OINTMENTS AND LIP BALM

THE PROCESS FOR MAKING THESE THREE ARE SIMILAR. THEY ARE A COMBINATION OF OIL AND WAX, ALTHOUGH THE PROPORTIONS OF EACH ARE A BIT DIFFERENT. SALVES AND LIP BALM WILL CONTAIN MORE WAX. OINTMENTS TEND TO CONTAIN LESS.

INGREDIENTS:

- 3T BEESWAX
- 2 OZ OLIVE OIL
- 1 OZ ST. JOHN'S WORT OIL
- 2 tsp COCONUT BUTTER
- 2 tsp COCOA BUTTER
- 1 VITAMIN E CAPSULE

TOOLS:

- CONTAINERS (GLASS/METAL POTS, PLASTIC TUBES)
- 1 CHOPSTICK
- 1 SAUCEPAN
- 1 PYREX GLASS MEASURING CUP
- HOT PLATE OR STOVETOP

DIRECTIONS:
ADD ALL INGREDIENTS TO PYREX GLASS CUP. PLACE 2" OF WATER IN THE SAUCEPAN AND HEAT ON STOVETOP. PLACE GLASS CUP IN THE WATER AND STIR MIXTURE WITH CHOPSTICK UNTIL DISSOLVED. POUR INTO GLASS, PLASTIC OR METAL CONTAINERS. COOL FOR 1 HOUR AND ENJOY!

LIP BALM

Aromatherapy

AROMATHERAPY IS THE USE OF <u>ESSENTIAL</u> <u>OILS</u> TO EFFECT A CHANGE IN THE MIND, BODY, EMOTIONS, AND/OR ETHERIC BODY THROUGH ACTIVE CHEMICALS FOUND IN THE PLANT.

GREAT CARE SHOULD BE TAKEN WHEN EXPERIMENTING WITH ESSENTIAL OILS. AT CERTAIN DOSES THEY CAN RENDER THE SKIN PHOTO-SENSITIVE (PRONE TO BURNS), DERMO-TOXIC (A RASH DEVELOPS) OR MUCOSAL IRRITATION CAN OCCUR. THAT SAID, START OUT WITH LOW DOSES AND DILUTE IN A CARRIER OIL.

<u>CARRIER OILS</u> – THESE ARE FATTY (COLD PRESSED)
SUBSTANCES THAT DILUTE ESSENTIAL OILS FOR EASE OF USE + SAFETY.
GOOD ONES TO TRY:

- COCONUT OIL
- GRAPE SEED OIL
- SHEA BUTTER
- ALMOND OIL

<u>ESSENTIAL OILS</u> – THESE ARE THE
DISTILLED AROMATIC MOLECULES (NOT WATER SOLUBLE) OF THE PLANT. AMONG OTHER ACTIONS, THIS IS THE PLANT'S IMMUNE SYSTEM. OUT OF ALL THE PLANTS ON EARTH, ONLY ABOUT 10% CONTAIN ESSENTIAL OILS. IN THE AYURVEDIC SYSTEM OF HEALING THESE OILS ARE CONSIDERED VATA. IT'S NO MISTAKE THAT THEY ARE BALANCED WITH **KAPHA** CARRIER OILS.

LIPO PH

HYDI PHO

34

AROMATHERAPY

IT IS POSSIBLE TO CATEGORIZE ESSENTIAL
OILS INTO 6 MAIN GROUPS. EACH
GROUP HAS A SET OF DISTINCT
CHARACTERISTICS AND PROPERTIES.

CITRUS OILS

- LEMON
- LIME
- ORANGE
- GRAPEFRUIT
- TANGERINE

PROPERTIES

- MOOD UPLIFTING
- ANTI-ANXIETY
- PHOTO TOXIC
- DERMO TOXIC
- CAN BE INGESTED IN
  SMALL AMOUNTS

CULINARY OILS

- OREGANO
- THYME
- BASIL
- TULSI
- ROSEMARY

- ANTI-MICROBIAL
- ANTI-BACTERIAL
- DIGESTIVE

RESPIRATORY OILS

- SPRUCE
- PINE
- FIR
- PINON
- EUCALYPTUS

- REDUCES THE MICROBIAL
  PATHOGENS IN THE AIR
- BALANCING TO THE
  UPPER RESPIRATORY
  SYSTEM
- DECONGESTANT
- LOW DERMO-TOXICITY
- FOR COLDS/FLU

FLORAL OILS

- ROSE
- LAVENDER
- GERANIUM
- PALMAROSA
- CLARY SAGE
- HELICHRYSUM
- JATAMANSI
- CHAMOMILE

- SUPPORTS AND BALANCES
  GLANDULAR SYSTEM
- ADRENAL SUPPORT
- THYROID SUPPORT
- PROMOTES SLEEP AND
  RELAXATION
- ANTI-INFLAMMATORY
- GENTLE
- ANTI-ANXIETY

ESSENTIAL OILS

SPICE OILS

GINGER
CINNAMON
CARDAMOM
BLACK PEPPER
CLOVE

properties

- DIGESTIVE
- ANALGESIC
- MUCO-LYTIC
- ANTI-MICROBIAL
- ANTI-BACTERIAL
- DECONGESTANT
- WARMING

SPIRITUAL OILS

FRANKINCENSE
MYRRH
PAOLO SANTO
SANDALWOOD

- PROMOTES A SENSE
  OF RELAXATION +
  WELL BEING
- SUPPORTS A MEDITATIVE
  STATE.
- FOR PURIFICATION

AROMATHERAPY ESSENTIALS

* ALL ESSENTIAL OIL BOTTLES SHOULD HAVE
   A SPILL PROOF DROP DISPENSER.

CHOOSE TO WORK WITH A FEW OILS
OF GOOD QUALITY FROM REPUTABLE
COMPANIES RATHER THAN MANY
LESS EXPENSIVE OILS, WHICH COULD
BE COMPROMISED BY PETROLEUM
BY-PRODUCTS.

- FLORACOPEIA
- AURA CACIA
- YOUNG LIVING
- SUN ROSE AROMATICS
- ENFLEURAGE

HOW DO WE USE THE OILS?
AROMATHERAPY APPLICATIONS:

1. BATH
2. STEAM INHALATION
3. MASSAGE (FACE, BODY, FEET/HANDS)
4. DIRECT PALM INHALATION
5. PERFUME
6. INTERNAL USE

1. **BATH** — ADD 5-15 DROPS OF ESSENTIAL OILS TO ANY OF THE FOLLOWING BASES.

   - **HONEY** - 2 TABLESPOONS
   - **MILK** - ¼ CUP
   - **SALT** - HANDFUL OR TWO

   ADD TO THE BATHTUB. THEN FILL WITH HOT WATER. SOAK FOR AT LEAST ½ HOUR.

CLEARING BATH SALTS

1 C.	SEA SALT
5 DROPS	PEPPERMINT OIL
5 DROPS	CLARY SAGE OIL
2 DROPS	ROSEMARY OIL
¼ tsp.	COCONUT OIL

A FEW FRESH WILD ROSE PETALS (IN SEASON)

ADD ALL INGREDIENTS TO A RE-PURPOSED GLASS FOOD JAR. SHAKE WELL. MAKES ENOUGH FOR 2 BATHS.

2. STEAM INHALATION

BOIL A FEW PINTS OF WATER.
POUR THE WATER IN A LARGE
GLASS OR CERAMIC BOWL.

ADD 5-10 DROPS OF A SINGLE
ESSENTIAL OIL OR A BLEND OF
4 OILS MAXIMUM.

PLACE YOUR HEAD ABOUT 6"
FROM THE WATER SO YOU CAN
EXPERIENCE THE AROMA VIA THE STEAM.

ENJOY INHALING + EXHALING
FOR 5-10 MINUTES.

*CAUTION, DO NOT ATTEMPT TO TOUCH
THE WATER WITH ANY PART OF YOUR
SKIN, AS IT IS 212°F AND VERY HOT.

3. MASSAGE

MAKING YOUR OWN MASSAGE OIL:
2 TABLESPOONS OF ANY
CARRIER OIL (COCONUT, GRAPESEED, ETC.)
20 DROPS OF ESSENTIAL OIL

* MASSAGE A LOVED ONE
* HANDS + FEET ARE PARTICULARY
EFFECTIVE PLACES FOR SELF-
MASSAGE. THE FEET HAVE THE
ABILITY TO ABSORB ESSENTIAL
OILS QUICKLY INTO THE SKIN
AND THE BLOOD STREAM.

4. DIRECT PALM INHALATION

PLACE 1 DROP OF AN ESSENTIAL
OIL (WITH THE EXCEPTION OF CITRUS OILS)
ON THE CENTER OF ONE PALM.
RUB BOTH PALMS TOGETHER.
CUP HANDS OVER YOUR NOSE
AND MOUTH. **INHALE** DEEPLY.
OPEN CUPPED HANDS, **EXHALE**..
REPEAT 5-6 TIMES.

5. INGESTING ESSENTIAL OILS

* WHEN IN DOUBT, DO NOT TAKE
ESSENTIAL OILS INTERNALLY
BECAUSE OF THE POSSIBILITY OF
MUCOSAL IRRITATION AND DEGRADATION

* THAT SAID, THERE ARE SOME THAT
MAY BE INGESTED IN TINY
AMOUNTS ONLY FROM UNADULTERATED
SOURCES (YOUNG LIVING OR FLORACOPEIA)

MINT RICE MILK

½ C. RICE MILK
1 DROP PEPPERMINT OR SPEARMINT OIL
* MIX WELL AND DRINK.

CITRUS SODA

1 CUP OF SELTZER WATER
1 drop of CITRUS OIL
(ORANGE, GRAPEFRUIT, LEMON, LIME)
* POUR SELTZER INTO A GLASS.
ADD 1 DROP OF OIL AND STIR.

6. PERFUME for THE BODY
CAN BE OIL OR ALCOHOL BASED

PERFUME OIL
1 DRAM JOJOBA OIL

¼ DRAM YOUR CHOICE OF
ESSENTIAL OILS

(BUY OR REPURPOSE A FEW DRAM SIZE
TINY GLASS BOTTLE TO USE FOR
MAKING + MIXING PERFUME OILS)

WHICH OILS? HOW MANY?
↳ TRY A *floral* OR EARTHY OR CITRUS.

BLEND A COMBINATION
OF A FEW DIFFERENT
CATEGORIES. GO TO THE
HEALTH FOOD STORE AND
TEST ALL OF THE SAMPLES.
WRITE DOWN THE ONES
THAT YOU LIKE BEST.

* LABEL YOU
CUSTOM BLE

ALCOHOL BASED PERFUME
IN A 2 OZ GLASS SPRAY BOTTLE
1 ¾ OZ ALCOHOL
20 DROPS SINGLE ESSENTIAL OIL
OR A BLEND
1 tsp GLYCERINE

E.G.
3 DROPS SANDALWO
3 DROPS VETIVER
5 DROPS JATAMA
5 DROPS MYRRH

♡ IF YOU EVER EXPERIENCE REDNESS,
BURNING, OR ITCHING ON THE SKIN FROM
AN ESSENTIAL OIL, <u>DO NOT</u> RINSE WITH
WATER. INSTEAD, DILUTE THE AREA WITH
LARGE AMOUNTS OF A CARRIER OIL
LIKE COCONUT OIL OR ALMOND OIL.

RINCIPLES for GOOD HEALTH

1. GET ADEQUATE SLEEP ~ 8 HRS per NIGHT.

2. REMOVE SYNTHETIC CHEMICALS FROM THE DIET, SKIN CARE, CLOTHING, AND CLEANING SUPPLIES.

3. DO SOME FORM OF EXERCISE EACH DAY.

4. SPEND TIME IN NATURE. GO TO THE PARK, WOODS, GARDEN, WILD-LIFE SANCTUARY, BEACH, LAKE, OCEAN, RIVER, MOUNTAIN, ETC.

5. HAVE A SET OF RITUALS + CEREMONIES THAT YOU CAN CALL UPON for GROUNDING OR UPLIFTING QUALITIES.
   (e.g. BURNING WHITE SAGE OR INCENSE,
   BREWING A POT OF TEA,
   CHANTING A MANTRA,
   TAKING A BATH, ETC.)

6. BE AWARE OF AND TAKE TIME TO BE IN: ALPHA STATES – JOY + PLEASURE
   THETA STATES – DEEP RELAXATION

7. MEDITATE (SEATED, STANDING, WALKING)

8. FOCUS ON KEEPING THE FREQUENCY + VIBRATION OF YOUR CELLS HIGH.

9. MAINTAIN A POSITIVE OUTLOOK ON LIFE.

BACTERIA + OTHER
helpful MICROBES

WE LIVE IN AN AGE WHERE BACTERIA HELPFUL TO THE HUMAN BODY COMPETE FOR SPACE IN, ON, AND AROUND THE BODY. CERTAIN CHEMICALS LIKE TRICLOSAN FOUND IN ANTI-BACTERIAL SOAPS ARE PARTLY RESPONSIBLE, CLEARING OUT COLONIES OF "HUMAN HELPERS" THAT PERFORM AN ARRAY OF DUTIES SUCH AS EATING + DIGESTING WHAT OUR BODIES ALONE CANNOT PROCESS. PESTICIDES ALSO KILL OFF SOME OF OUR MINI-FRIENDS AS WELL (ONE MORE REASON TO BUY ORGANIC).

THE ANTI-DOTE TO THE ANTI-BACTERIAL OBSESSION EXISTS IN CLEAR SIGHT. FERMENTED FOODS CONTAIN NUMEROUS MICRO-ORGANISMS THAT WILL RE-POPULATE ENVIRONMENTS THAT HAVE BEEN OCCUPIED BY "SPACE INVADERS". RAW KOMBUCHA CONTAINS A COAGULATED MASS THAT IS PART OF A "S.C.O.B.Y." IT STANDS FOR SYMBIOTIC COLONY OF BACTERIA AND YEAST. THIS WILL HELP RE-OCCUPY OUR GUTS.

NATTO	SAURKRAUT	TEMPEH	
TAMARI	PICKLES	BEER	FERMENTED
MISO	KOMBUCHA	WINE	ALLIES
YOGURT	KEFIR	OLIVES	

BIBLIOGRAPHY

HEALING WISE, SUSUN WEED. ASH TREE
   PUBLISHING: 1989.

OPENING OUR WILD HEARTS TO THE
   HEALING HERBS, GAIL FAITH EDWARDS.
   ASH TREE PUBLISHING : 2000.

HERBAL HEALING FOR WOMEN, ROSEMARY
   GLADSTAR. FIRESIDE: 1993.

AN ASTROLOGICAL HERBAL FOR WOMEN,
   ELIZABETH BROOKE. CROSSING PRESS:
   1995.

THE NEW AGE HERBALIST, RICHARD MABEY.
   FIRESIDE: 1988

HERBAL THERAPY FOR WOMEN, ELIZABETH
   BROOKE. THORSONS: 1992.

PLANT SPIRIT HEALING, PAM MONTGOMERY.
   BEAR & COMPANY: 2008.

HEALING MAGIC, ROBIN ROSE BENNETT.
   STERLING: 2004.

HERBAL FOR THE CHILDBEARING YEAR,
   SUSUN WEED. ASH TREE PUBLISHING:
   1986.

WEEDS HEAL, ISLA BURGESS.
   CAXTON PRESS : 1998.

EARTHWISE HERBAL, MATT WOOD
      NORTH ATLANTIC BOOKS: 2009.

SUBSCRIBE!

For as little as $13/month, you
can support a small, independent
publisher and get every book that we
publish—delivered to your doorstep!

www.Microcosm.Pub/BFF